Porridge

Porridge

Winner of the Press 53 Award for Poetry

Prose Poems

Richard Garcia

Press 53
Winston-Salem

Press 53, LLC
PO Box 30314
Winston-Salem, NC 27130

First Edition

A TOM LOMBARDO POETRY SELECTION

Cover design by Kevin Morgan Watson

Author photo by Dinah Berland

Printed on acid-free paper
ISBN 978-1-941209-35-6

For Katherine

Acknowledgments

Grateful acknowledgment is made to the editors of the following print and online journals, in which these poems first appeared, sometimes in a different form or with different titles:

Black Warrior Review, "The Show"
Cease, Cows, "Room Seven" and "The Next New Thing"
The Más Tequila Review, "While You Were Out," "The
    Future," and "The Rising"
One, "Awake"
Rat's Ass Review, "Thinkology"
Solstice, "Diorama"
Spillway, "One Morning" and "Breathe"
Ultraviolet Tribe, "And So it Was"
Wherewithal, "The Tontlawald" and "The Juniper Tree"

—◈—

"The Aloha Shirt" is for Steve Heller
"Blue" is for Peggy Dobreer
"Huntington Botanical Gardens, Pasadena" is for Brigit
    Pegeen Kelly
"While You Were Out" is for Katherine Williams
"Yellow" is for Judith Pacht

"Breathe" is after Paul Klee
"Dark Matter Here" is after John Hollander
"The Show" is after Donald Barthelme

And thanks also to the fellowship of The Long Table Poets
of Charleston, South Carolina.

Table of Contents

Introduction
by Tom Lombardo
Poetry Series Editor

As I judged the 2016 Press 53 Award for Poetry—reading submissions of poetry manuscripts from April through October 2015—I came across this wonderful and mysterious collection of prose poems entitled *Porridge.* At first reading, I was impressed by the excellent examples of the fable form of this sub-genre, first popularized by the 19th Century French Symbolists Charles Baudelaire, Stéphane Mallarmé, Paul Verlaine, and Arthur Rimbaud.

As in the recent work of prose poets like Russell Edson, Shivani Mehta, and others, the prose poems in this particular submission were magically fantastical, time-suspended stories with incredible leaps of death-defying logic like a trapeze troupe in a circus. In the poet's take on the Estonian folk tale "A Tale of the Tontlawald" (p. 39) we meet a young boy who becomes central to the *Porridge* narrative.

> Reading the story the boy looked over his
> shoulder and realized the book was closing,
> taking the evening with it. Soon it would be
> dark, and he was alone in the forest.

The young boy then experiences darkly Gothic adventures that lead him to a confrontation with "selfish trees" with "poisonous seeds" and "small lakes . . . high up in the canopies of the forest," all of which force him away from home, the doll that had been left in his place never spoke or closed its eyes. Facing the uncertainties of growing up, this young boy begins his journey toward maturation.

Upon my second and third readings of *Porridge*, I continued to enjoy this submission—at the time one of the more intriguing of the 294 anonymous entries into the Press 53 competition. I was clearly fascinated by these amazing fables. I came to comprehend that this particular submission bore a set of deeply hidden metaphors that set up a collection-length narrative—an autobiography—of a young boy who struggles with growing up in an incomprehensible world to become a mature man who ages into his middle years, struggling to make sense of his life. The metaphors took me—the sole reader of all the submissions—on a life-long narration that begins with the carefree, almost accidental naiveté of a young boy to the man who matures in a world that doesn't always conform to his expectations to the older gentleman's wondrous nostalgia tinged with regret at the onrushing approach of the inevitable. Over a half-dozen readings, *Porridge* became for me the view of *a life*, with a theme that no matter what we do in this life, we do it alone, and each of us must come to some sort of understanding, individually and alone, of what it all means.

As the narrator of *Porridge* realizes that there are many paths he could have taken to his current point in time, he explores the many identities he might have fallen into.

> Lost at Bloomindale's, the boy wanders. He finds himself in Lingerie among the unmentionables . . . he rides the Down escalator . . . he looks up, and across from him there is another boy who looks exactly like him on another escalator . . . They smile at each other as they descend on their separate journeys.

—"The Unmentionables" p. 55

Life may split into several directions. Sometimes we have a choice, as in Robert Frost's "The Road Not Taken," sometimes we don't, as in the boy lost in Lingerie, and *Porridge* made me as a reader wonder: Do we all have doppelgangers who travel those roads not taken by us? And if so, how do they fare?

The boy becomes a man, another step on his escalator in which the vagaries of chance play a role, demonstrated figuratively by an incident at a wedding. The wedding toppers—the bride and groom figurines atop the wedding cake—topple to the floor after a disastrous cake accident. As in a fairy tale, the figurines come to life, and run off to first live in a closet, then in a shoe, and finally in "a nice cottage in a snow globe," a fabled leap into one of many alternate universes.

Later in the collection, the narrator as an older man confronts how the random chance of circumstance remains a mystery. He uses a children's nursery rhyme to develop a list of similes that end with this regretful memory:

> Like a road sign in a ditch: Slow . . . Children
> . . . Playing. And here I am, not remembering
> the name of the wind that brought me here.

—"Like a Crooked Man" p. 52.

Deeper into the collection, you will discover, as I did, fables that search for meaning as the aging narrator confronts his inevitable fate.

> The future was fun while it lasted. But it was
> soon eclipsed by the distant past. Or perhaps
> it had become the ever after.

—"The Future" p. 47

As my continued reading of submissions over the Summer of 2015 moved *Porridge* into the 25 semi-finalists and then into the 10 finalists, my judgment of these individual prose poems overcame their individuality, and I became quite certain of their lyrical unity. I understood the subjective view of a life lived and the perspective gained as the endpoint of such a life rushes forward. It's a combination of nostalgia, regret, and pure wonder that the poet had woven into the fabric of *Porridge*.

> Bring back the roll top desk. Bring back inkwells. And ink, and fountain pens. Don't bring back Mrs. Tucker, my fourth grade teacher leaning over me as I practice my penmanship. Bring back the letter that comes in the mail . . . And eternity. Whatever happened to eternity? Bring back eternity.

—"Bring Back" p. 57

Along the way to eternity, *Porridge* presents other fabulist, allusive tales that delighted me in the manner of all good prose poems: a rhetorical battle of one-upmanship between God and Satan that keeps popping up unexpectedly; the practical impacts of the numeral 7 that range from 1950's crooner Perry Como to a dwarf, Snarky, who was rejected by Disney casting agents for *Snow White*; and several historical artifacts viewed in completely new light poetically like Vasko Popa or the deadly Hartford Circus fire of 1944. And finally, the answer to my constant musing as I read *Porridge* over and over: just what is porridge?

The poet turned out to be the accomplished prose poet Richard Garcia, who has published two collections of prose poetry, *The Chair* and *Chickenhead*, and has included prose poems in other collections. He has used the fable form—a thoroughly enjoyable and uniquely dark form of entertainment—to shed light on a serious topic: How does one bring back eternity? Perhaps the answer to that question is buried in the alternate takes on history, cosmology, and creation myths that Garcia has stirred into this *Porridge.*

I am honored and excited to present to readers *Porridge* by Richard Garcia, the winner of the 2016 Press 53 Award for Poetry. I'm certain you will enjoy it as much as I did.

Porridge

Little Miss Blonde Breaking-and-Entering. Lock-picker. She touched our chairs. She lay in our beds. Burn it. Burn it all. Dad says we shall return to the forest. Pack nothing. Take nothing. In time, we shall forget. Forget the candles on the table. The gauze curtains and the windowsills, the window boxes with their small blue flowers. Forget the spoon and the warm white bowl.

Little Red Goldilocks

Little Red Goldilocks walks along a forest path. A wolf loiters at the crossroads. Hey, little girl, he says to Little Red Goldilocks, What fine looking hair you have, what a nice red hood. He is about to offer her a ride on his back, but he hears the dogs baying in the distance—the dogs, those betrayers that have learned how to bark, how to obey. The wolf turns and trots away, slipping deeper into the forest. Little Red Goldilocks was about to ask him, Kind Sir, where are those cuddly bears, where is their little cottage? She hears the dogs getting closer, the shouts and cries of the men beating the bushes with sticks, stomping, coming closer. She leaves the path and makes her way toward the whisper of running water.

The Teller

Letting the wick be overcome by darkness, the tale unwound. Hoof-beats, a single horse and rider. The night bird that never sings at night did not sing that night. There was someone at the gate, someone at the door. He wore a mask, his horse wore a mask, even his dog wore a mask. Once upon a time this is the end of my tale. How did I know the dog ate all the gruel? Because I was under the table when the witch turned into a wizard and the wizard became a hummingbird that rose into the vaulted ceiling and shot out a tiny window faster than. . . . And I, the teller who told you this, forget everything I told you. I tell you no lie.

Field

I find myself in a playing field of some kind. But I don't know what the game is. I seem to be the only player. I feel guilty, as if I have something I should do but don't know what. Am I late? Am I early? Am I a goalie or a scorekeeper? Maybe the mascot? Maybe I'm *it*? That's it—everyone is hiding and I have to find them. Or I am hiding and they have to find me. Maybe everyone forgot about the game and went home but I am still hiding. I cup my hands to my mouth, Come out, come out, wherever you are. I wrap my arms around my shoulders as far as I can and caress myself. If anyone is standing behind me they will think I am making out with a fair maiden. Or a beautiful princess. A blonde maybe.

Invocation

And the fathers come home with their black lunch pails, khaki pants, sweat-stained shirts. The Fuller Brush man packs up his display case as night approaches. The brush for sweeping crumbs away. The brush for brushing silken hair at bedtime. And the mothers stand on the stoops, lean out the windows, call the boys home. But the boys do not listen to the mothers calling. The mothers beat pots with wooden spoons. One mother rattles a soup ladle around a cowboy dinner triangle. One mother taps a milk bottle with a carving fork. The mothers call and rattle and clang and clang. Only one boy, Sheldon, always a good boy, runs Wee-wee-wee all the way home.

Huntington Botanical Gardens, Pasadena

Soon after we pay and enter the garden, I kneel down by the koi pond. A dragonfly with transparent wings buzzes over us. A tiny frog plops off a lily pad. Bees circle the lotus blossoms. I invite the child to sit with me. With my lips in an O, I make little popping bubble sounds. The koi, the white, golden, striped and spotted koi rise to the surface and swim toward us. They slide out of the water on to the muddy rim of the pond and make O's with their mouths as if in greeting or perhaps they are practicing breathing on land. I show the child how to break pieces of bread and feed them to the koi. Carefully, with one finger we touch the koi and they do not seem to mind. It is a warm winter day and I carry my flannel shirt. We stroll on the grass between the statues. Because we do not have a ball, I tie a knot in my shirt and toss it to the boy. We run and jump about, each of us making up the rules of International Shirt-ball. If the statue of the warrior catches the ball with his spear it is ten points. If the shirt-ball bounces off the head of Mnemosyne, the Muse of Memory, we have to forget all the rules of International Shirt-ball and make up new ones. In the rainforest section of the garden we hold our noses at the death-stench of the carrion plant. And the timid mimosa folds its leaves when the boy strokes them. In the desert section we make shadows with our bodies over the soap plant and it goes to sleep. The garden is like one of his mother's poems. There are statues that seem to wrestle with the air. There are masks of joy and sorrow with water streaming from their mouths. And then the procession of a swarm of bees bearing the partially decomposed body of a snake drifts over the grass. It is getting dark, and the boy and I hide behind a statue of Diana the Huntress. We crouch down on all fours among her pack of dogs, hoping the security guards, who are making their final rounds before the gardens close, will not see us.

Belief

No one at the dinner party believes the man when he mentions Superman's Super Boner. They snort. They sneer—another one of his stories. He leaves the dinner party. His wife remains. He walks alone in the night. The streets are becoming unfamiliar. He is not surprised by the sudden appearance of the fog. It is his life, after all. There is always fog. But wait. Great Scott! Maybe it was Batman? *Gotham Gazette: Batman's Greatest Boner. Joker pulls boner of the Year . . . foiled by Batman. "So! They all laughed at my boner. I'll show them. Gotham City will rue the day. . . ."* The man thinks he can find his way back to the dinner party. In the Bat Library, Batman and Robin continue their study of the great boners of all time, and try to anticipate the Joker's next dastardly deed.

The Rising

It is said that the winding path of the forest leads into the sky. My companion is beginning to believe that she is the sky. The clouds are flagstones and we look forward to hopping from stone to stone. The real estate men mumble among themselves. The tent flaps its wings without achieving flight. My companion wants to become a wave instead. Not a real wave, not a greeting or goodbye, but one of those waves of the future as yet unseen, although trendy among the very few. The real estate men demand a refund. The tent cannot open its eyes or get out of bed. I am going somewhere or maybe not. My companion says, Come unto me with thine own self. The real estate men want to try out for the show. They envision a pageant or tableau of famous real estate lots. Hearing the news, the tent rises to the occasion.

And So It Was

Bored with the world and bored with each other, God and Satan made a new world. But it was a boring world. One day Eve came. Get me some magazines, she said to God. Get me some catalogues, she said to Satan. They were angry but said nothing. Who was this woman? Where did she come from? Each month when Eve got her magazines and catalogues she put God and Satan to work. They were grumpy but did as Eve bade. God would plant some forests. Satan would climb a big ladder and push bits of shiny stones into the night sky.

One Morning

Startled out of a dream one morning, a woman fell off the bed and noticed that she had acquired wings. She stood and looked at them in the mirror. She was disappointed to see that they were not really wings. They were metal strings and she had become a harp. A woman fell out of bed and noticed that she had become a harp. She remembered a distant thrum that must have been her body hitting the floor. She stood in front of the mirror, reached back, and tried to play herself. She could not. A woman was sad because she was a harp and could not play herself.

Under the Robinson Crusoe Umbrella

Sitting on the back porch with Blank Page. Listening to birds call from the trees. I don't know the names of the birds. I don't know the names of the trees. Or the bushes. Blank Page says, How about the names of the sky—I suppose you don't know any of the names of the sky, do you? True enough, Blank Page, I reply, I don't even know your real name. That's easy, Blank Page says—to you, my friend, and only to you, my name is Blankety-Blank-Blank-Blank Page.

Breathe

The terrible clatter of the twittering machine. There goes that one. Oh, here comes another one, complete with an archive of listeners. The listeners stir in the gallery. One coughs politely. An intensity of utensils. Now they rattle their utensils. Pay them and they will go away. But it is not song or sixpence they want. You don't know their currency. Maybe they just want you to breathe.

Fact

It is possible to lead a cow upstairs, but not down. Few people are aware of this. Not so, says the blue snow globe. What do you know, I reply, You should taste like grape jelly. And you, the snow globe says, Should not be talking to an inanimate object. Should not be placing the tip of your tongue against cold glass. Meanwhile, that bird that only sings in the morning sings—a bubbly chirping, something like bubbles popping. But it's always night inside the snow globe. Night over the village inside the snow globe and the houses sleep. And the houses sleep under a blanket of snow.

Spindle

I have seen you from time to time, over the years—in fact, yesterday, I wandered through the dark tunnel under the Dock Street Theater—cracked plaster over brick, chessboard path etched with cirrus flourishes, what the guidebooks call the Secret Passageway—emerged, shielding my eyes, palm against the wall, stunned for a moment by the late afternoon sunlight of the courtyard—and there you were, smiling to yourself, head bent, concentrating on your spindle, winding, unwinding a ball of yarn. Without looking up, you spoke my name, as if you had been waiting for me.

Bear

There was a bear riding on a train. He fell from the moving train. Or was he pushed? That rude boot. There was a bear that leapt from a train. He crossed a field into a forest. Where is my dinner? There was a bear that found berries. Red berries, purple berries, a little stream, and look, a lake—fish, and sometimes honey. There was a bear that fell or was pushed off a moving train. Did he escape? Or had he just retired? Life was easy now. Easy as balancing on a barrel, as riding a tricycle while waving a little yellow flag.

Regret

God was depressed. Satan was depressed. They each had their regrets. These people they had made were disappointing. They all wanted to be animals—they ate, grew, nested, copulated, reproduced—animals! So God and Satan summoned Lilith, Eve's older sister. She came in a black Cadillac convertible driven by an enormous serpent, accompanied by angels. One angel wore a leather jacket. One picked his teeth with a switchblade. Another angel, dressed in a zoot suit made of small mirrors, seemed preoccupied with his fingernails. Lilith wore her little black dress. Now we're getting somewhere, said God. Satan nodded, Yeah, baby.

Vasko Popa

Attention all departments: the computer wants you to save everything. It is compiling a history of the universe. That's all it is, you know, a verse: Uni—one. One furrow of the plough out and back again. Attention all departments: Vasko Popa is coming. He will ask you a question. Do you like white or red wine? Say red. Pay no attention to his translator. He is working for a government agency. Contract spy, *agent provocateur*. Vasko Popa is coming. He will ask you a question. What became of the cow that was sold for five beans? You will have one chance to answer. Just one.

The Wedding Toppers

A bride and groom, two figurines, topped a wedding cake. After the wedding photographer had backed into the cake to try to get a better shot of the lucky couple, they never saw the rest of the wedding. The cake and photographer had fallen together. The bride and groom were both well-known poets and each had their own stalker who came to each of their weddings. After the cake fell, one stalker's hand plunged through the cake after the toppers but they escaped into a closet, where they found a large shoe to live in. It was crowded in the shoe and after seven years the landlady asked them to leave. The wedding toppers found a nice cottage in a snow globe to live in. They would stand at the window of the cottage and marvel at the snow. They knew it was not real snow but that was fine with them. The snow fell on the front lawn, on the picket fence. It lay quietly on the mailbox. Not a real mailbox.

The People

The People come into the valley, dragging the bones of their dead wrapped in the leaves of large vines. They believe that if they plant them in the right place, new people will grow. They are planting them in our gardens; it is our nature to help them. The vines sprout and climb with mechanical speed. They are covering the walls of our houses, covering the windows, entangling doors, roofs and towers. The People never look at the night sky. They fear our enormous stone pillars that vibrate at the frequency of the stars. It will take The People a hundred years to bury them.

The Showing

He opened the cellar door. Cellar door, he said, the most beautiful word in the English language. I wondered, is it two words or one? What about celadon or saltcellar? He led me, exaggerating his limp it seemed to me, from room to room, although in the catalogue, they were referred to as cells, each one complete with a cot, a blanket, a billet, and a candle. Was I too old for the student life? I asked with uncharacteristic boldness, What about the grotto? Maybe, for a few more florins . . .? Ah, he said, looking up at me, then down, perhaps gauging my threadbare look, the holes in my knickers and my ragged cloak— was that poverty, or style? Yes, of course, he whispered, pulling on my arm, his dark eyes glowing darker, The grotto, with its luminescent stalactites, its underground river, and the pool where you can float in the dark with schools of tiny, transparent fish brushing against your skin.

Thinkology

I think crows are smart. Like Hector. He's a crow. He sits on my shoulder and whispers into my ear, The sum of the square roots of any two sides of an isosceles triangle is equal to the square root of the remaining side. I think I could scatter myself all around you. I think I could jump into the wind for you. You think if I had half a brain, I would stay away from you. You say, Honey, I am fire, and you are straw, stay away from me. But hey, I have a brain, I do, I even have a degree in thinkology, and I say, Baby, I'm made of straw, and straw was made to burn.

The Juniper Tree

My two brothers are sparrows in the juniper tree. My two sisters are branches of the juniper tree. Go and find my head, one brother says to me. Go and find my body, says the other brother. My two sisters remain silent. Or maybe the leaves of the tree are speaking too loud to the wind. When the wind pauses I hear one sister say, Go and find my birthday cupcake, the one with the single candle that Mother gave to me. Go and find my pearl earring, the other sister says, the one I left under my pillow. Now the leaves of the juniper tree are opening and closing—I only hear the juniper tree. The juniper tree is amused at something the wind says—the wind, that world traveler, so suave, so blasé.

Almost Memory

July 6th, 1944, was a hot day in Hartford. Grandma does not remember the heat, or July 6th, 1944, or Hartford. But she does recall wavering things, dark swallows in the dusk, bats maybe, or the air all ash and feathers, sequins and embers in a baby-blue sky, and Uncle Remus. Black powder stains the kitchen sink. But will her wet wringing ever end? She wanted to go to the circus but Mama took her to see *Song of the South*. Zip-a-dee-doo-dah. July 6th, 1944, in Hartford. She remembers and does not remember the heat, singed wings, a sad-faced Willy the Clown trying to mop up fire.

Escaped Babies

Alarmed by a lullaby he hears over and over about a falling cradle, a baby crawls away from a hospital nursery. He finds a cardboard box in an alley and lives in it. Soon he is joined by other escaped babies. They will be coming for us soon, the first escaped baby says. And it is true. Grownups are looking for them. Nurses, orderlies, schoolteachers, truant officers and policemen are looking for them. Soon there are more escaped babies—escaped babies everywhere. Hanging on to the rear platforms of streetcars, throwing rocks at the Junior Museum, stealing milk bottles from front stoops, climbing trees and telephone poles. They beat their chests and crow like roosters from the rooftops.

Awake

Stumbling in my eighth grade social studies classroom, I collided with Karen Jungnickle—my hands, accidentally, at the height of her breasts. I did not have time to caress them because we passed right through each other and found ourselves in another galaxy. Karen and I stood there, in the vapor trail of a comet, stunned, suddenly awake, like after we had seen Elvis on *The Ed Sullivan Show.* Then we were in a forest, walking hand-in-hand along a path, making our way back to the social studies classroom. Karen wondered about the breadcrumbs. How had they lasted so long on the path? I wondered about the crows that crouched on the branches. Why were they so silent?

Seven

Perry Como was the seventh son of a seventh son. He was born with seven hundred dollars crunched up in his tiny fist. He was an heir to the Seven Cities of Cibola and privy to the seven missing years of Jesus. He had seven cardigan sweaters, which he wore, successively, in each of his seven Christmas specials. He was a precursor to Mister Rogers, who was also a seventh son of a seventh son. When Perry Como met Mister Rogers, the seven sleepers rolled over in their sleep, their seven-league boots all lined up; their seven little caps hanging on the seven pegs trembled in a wind that blew into their cave. Perry Como opened the seventh holiday present. Someday soon, he thought, Surely, the seven brides shall dance, reunited with the seven brothers.

Blue

Peggy did not want to be born. She hid in her mother's ribcage. Then she fell through the slats into churning water that carried her away. She woke in a city of the future where no one lived. There was a clock on a tower that ran backwards. In the distance she heard a train. Or perhaps someone was playing a large harmonica. Because in a former life a forest troll had kissed her, she loved the color blue. Her mother loved it too. They would sit on the pavement in a vacant lot. Peggy heard voices from another country no one else could hear. What do they say, her mother would ask. Peggy knew, whatever the voices said, it was not true. So she made something up. She said, The voices say blue, blue, blue, once and forever, blue.

The Loft Party

The Birdman had not been invited but came in
costume because a costume party would be easy to
crash. He leaned over The Twins, trying not to whisk
them with his wing, and asked, Who is that man
standing in the center of the room looking so puzzled?
The Twins were not really twins at all. They were called
The Twins because they always spoke in unison. Or
were, as at this moment, mournfully silent in unison.
It was The Forgetter who stood in the center of the
room, a loft in downtown Los Angeles, and people
whom he seemed to know but whose names he could
not remember navigated around him as if he were a
post driven into the middle of the room. The Forgetter
did remember one moment. He considered writing a
treatise, a philosophical or scientific treatise. It would
be about the moment he was stepping onto the freight
elevator on the way up to the loft party. Or something
about the slats of the wooden gate, they way the
shadow of the gate flashed on the concrete walls of
the shaft as it ascended to the top floor.

Waking Up

A prose poem woke up in an alley. He was lying on the pavement among trash bins, empty bottles, cigarette butts and the smell of urine. He raised his head and noticed the rear exits to buildings. He hadn't wanted to wake up as a prose poem. He coulda been a story. Maybe just a very short story, but at least something in which something happens. He coulda been a fight or a murder or a dying child, a beautiful woman who has forgotten her name, or a soldier coming back from the war. Something. He coulda been a book of related stories in which an unnamed character, one who played no actual part in the stories, would make an appearance in each story. Perhaps he would be the unnamed character sitting, unnoticed by anyone in the story, on a park bench. Or he would deliver the mail. Or you would see him glance from the window of a departing bus. The prose poem got on his feet and dusted off his pants and the front of his shirt. He needed a shave and his teeth felt scuzzy. He knew the rear doors to the buildings were not real doors. No one would be coming to the alley. No one would pick up the garbage. It was not a real alley, but maybe it was a story—the story of his blankety-blank-blank life. Nothing would happen. He wouldn't be doing whatever he would be doing if he were a story instead of a prose poem. Damn.

The Porridge Eaters

The porridge eaters always mispronounce the word *please.* They wipe their mouths on the back of their hands. They wipe their hands on their trousers. If there is an intruder in the village, or a stumbling monster-man, the porridge eaters grumble, run and grab their torches, and then chase the monster-man. Where do they get those torches? Are they just lying around? How do they light them so easily? How do they stay lit in the misty fog? After they have chased the monster-man and failed to catch him, they return to the hovel and demand porridge. Exhausted after their grueling chase of the monster-man, they sit around the table. They clasp a wooden spoon in each fist and pound the table in unison, chanting, Pease porridge hot, pease porridge cold . . . .

Yellow

When Judith opened her eyes in her first dream, she saw a wild dog chase a rabbit. She was the rabbit and she hid on top of her mother's head. What a nice hat, her mother said about the rabbit on her head. The wild dog, confused, stopped to admire the hat. This was in New York, and The Great Depression was learning how to dance. Judith's first steps were dance steps, a toddler's version of the Lindy Hop. Ladders were learning to swing-dance to the pleasant tapping of neighborhood typewriters. Woodwinds lined up in the hallway waiting their turn on the living room floor. They stretched, made sure their dance shoes were laced tight. Slowly, her mother went to sleep, ignoring the woodwinds and the clatter of ladders. The rabbit went to sleep. The wild dog went to sleep. Judith went to sleep. They all dreamed of yellow. Judith woke believing she had invented a special kind of yellow, a deep yellow, like the blaring of a trombone at midnight. Someday, the wild dog whispered in her ear as Judith drew spirals in her Etch-a-Sketch, You shall instruct whirlwinds in proper manners. You shall be famous for the marvelous soup, the soup named by the *New York Times*, The Everything-that-Anyone-Ever-Wanted Soup, the soup fabled in story and song, the soup that shall abide in your refrigerator, steadfast.

Rejected Dwarf

Years later, Snarky, one of the original Seven Dwarfs
rejected from the Seven Dwarfs casting call, is still
steaming over it. Like they are doing a movie of his
life but now he's too old to play himself except for the
death scene. So fifty years later Snarky is still sitting
each night in the dark bar at Musso & Frank's. They
keep a milk crate that helps him climb onto the stool.
Closing time, and Frank calls for a cab. Did I tell you
that Snow White had sex with all the Seven Dwarfs
except Droopy? And Frank says, Yeah, Snarky, you
tell me every night. I'm telling ya, Snarky says, It musta
been 'cause there was a spot of cum on my tie. It
mighta been the way I looked at the script girl. But
I'm telling you the truth, I swear, my hands have a life
of their own. Out on a date with Walt's secretary I
tried to control them. As my left hand crept across
the table like an alien tarantula headed straight for her
cleavage, my right hand swatted at it with a rolled-up
copy of *Variety*. You know how that is. When you're
convinced that there is no way they will choose you.
And guess what, there is no way they will choose you.

Mortimer

A little mouse scurrying in my wastebasket. Mortimer. My old lady says, Flush it down the toilet. No way. I keep him in my pocket. Eventually, she throws us both out. We hit the rails. Nights at Sweeney's Boarding House, Mortimer falls asleep in my slipper while I tell him stories. Mortimer Buckaroo. Mortimer Saves the Day. I don't know how it happened, but one day he is gone. I look everywhere, even put an ad in the newspaper. A year later, I sneak into a movie theater to get out of the rain—there is Mortimer on screen. My Mortimer. He's a star—he's a buckaroo. He saves the day. I hitchhike to the studio. They won't let me in. I go back every day. But we're pals, I tell the guards, His real name is Mortimer. Every day I show them the slipper. This is his bed, I tell them. This is where he sleeps.

The Song

There was an old man who pushed a wagon he had made from parts of bicycles, baby carriages and wire. He had fastened a pair of car radio antennas to its handlebars, and attached to the antennas were wings made from the ribs of umbrellas and black plastic trash bags. The wings swung open and closed as he pushed along. But best was the chirpy ping of the song the spokes made when they brushed against some tines he had fashioned from aluminum cans. Whenever he passed, people would come out from wherever they were hiding to hear the song. It was a slow song because he could only push slow. But everyone who heard the song knew that if he could push faster it would still be the same song—just faster.

After

When your eyes open you'll ask, Is it tomorrow yet? Your attendant will smile but remain silent. Like when the bride lifts her veil and your eyes tear up, even though you are at the wrong wedding and have no idea who these people are. You will see Abraham Lincoln standing in a laundry hamper. Having once slept in a suitcase, you'll know just how he feels. And didn't you, as an infant, sleep in a glass coffin? You will search your pockets, your wallet, repeatedly, for a document that needs to be stamped before you can proceed. The carpet smells like bleach, as if someone tried to clean up a crime scene. You are waiting on a traffic safety island outside the bullring in Pamplona. Right now, concentrate. Your final instructions are to keep the mother of the groom from leaving the wedding too soon.

The Tontlawald

Reading the story the boy looked over his shoulder and realized the book was closing, taking the evening with it. Soon it would be dark, and he was alone in the forest. He had only read a page of the story and did not know what would happen next. He had always wanted to sleep in the hollowed-out shell of a tree that had been struck by lightning and had its inner core burnt out. He had read that some large trees were rather selfish. Their bark left a covering of chips on the ground that was poisonous to the seeds of any species of tree but their own. Were there really small lakes in hollows high up in the canopies of the forest? Would the old couple miss him at home? They seldom spoke, and if they did, it was in a language he did not speak. It might be years before they realized that the doll that had been left in his place never spoke or closed its eyes.

The Next New Thing

Martín the Dancing Bear had heard about The Next New Thing. The Next New Thing, he said, Will be here and gone and no one will ever know. The Next New Thing will be the smallest of all The Next New Things ever. I said I was The Next New Thing but The Inquisitor did not believe me. Meanwhile was only mean for a while. Then she showed me her collection of tangerine tango pumps. She showed me her tattoos of Celtic marauders. Finally The Next Thing arrived disguised as The Nurse with our three o'clock herbal tea and Thorazine. O, Next New Thing, you could not fool us, gathered around the credenza. You could not fool Hugo the Strong. You could not fool The Magic Cow. You could not fool The Scarecrow. You could not fool The Harp. Next New Thing, you are so tiny and we have waited for you so long, even The Apparition, if he could cry, would cry for you.

The Invisible Square Space

God and Satan were bored so they called Adam. Adam came running up, out of breath. God said to him, Take that boulder and roll it over there. Done. Then He said, Take that other boulder and roll it over there, across from the first stone. Done. God was pleased and about to say, Good, but Satan said, Wait, I've got an idea. He told Adam to roll another boulder, and then another. Now the four boulders enclosed an invisible square space. That's good, said God. What now? Satan asked. Then, spreading his arms in a grand gesture, God said, We could make another invisible square space on top of the first one, and another on top of that. Hmm, said Satan, Maybe so—and then we can build a huge wall around all of it.

Three

Four is such a bore. But three keeps us tripping, stumbling, perpetually off balance. There are three ways to go about this. This way. That way. And no way. Of course, we shall never know what *this* is. Or *that.* Here we stop, take hands, all three of us, brother, brother, and absent sister, and go around the mulberry bush Father planted. Go around the mulberry bush. Go around . . . so early in the morning.

The Inkwell

It is embarrassed by its status as a rare object. Beautiful earth-stained corrosion. What patina! Bronze, flecked blue, reminiscent of lapis lazuli or a continent of clouds breaking up over the ocean as seen by pilots of an airliner that has lost all contact with its base and destination. Blah, blah, the inkwell is brooding. Don't speak to it. It's in a bad mood.

The Pen

The pen remembers the inkwell, how staid, and the creamy parchment on which it slid along so effortlessly. The way the ink shimmered for a moment before it dried. The pen remembers the quill, its jaunty self-importance, its flirtatious flippancy. The pen remembers being lost. How its owner went from inn to inn asking wayfarers and pilgrims, Have you seen a pen, emerald green, speckled with tortoiseshell brilliances, a golden nib? The pen remembers bobbing into a little inlet, remembers nudging its owner's hand as his limp wrist dangled over a mossy bank. The pen remembers its owner waking and stepping into the stream to retrieve his pen. The pen remembers how it teased, seeming to float away downstream, then turned to circle its owner's shins three times. Circling three times, bobbing in the current, so happy.

Spoon

It is not true that the spoon ran off with the plate. It was all the plate's idea. The spoon was just along for the ride. The plate could hardly believe it. Looking down at the earth on the way to the moon, the earth was a giant plate. And the moon was a giant plate too. The spoon and the plate had many other adventures. The Spoon and the Plate in the Cave of the Seven Sleepers. The Spoon and the Plate Go Wild. The plate grew tired of the spoon. How it would bend to the will of any amateur psychic. How the spoon was sometimes so full, all Taste me, dripping honey. Sometimes the spoon was cold, empty, even cruel. Like a spoon filched by a prison inmate, hidden in a Gideon Bible, its handle ground down and sharpened into a killing-tool.

The Horn Bird

In the Forest of the Horn Bird the call of the horn bird is seldom heard. It does not call to alert of danger. It does not call to find its mate or locate its young. It calls for no reason, and if its call is answered it retreats further into the forest. The crystalline forest. The forest of metallic spires. The forest of petrified ash. The forest of dust suspended in midair. The forest of silica. The forest of rusted webs. The forest of crusted soot. The forest of ashes all fall down.

The Future

The future was fun while it lasted. But it was soon eclipsed by the distant past. Or perhaps it had become the ever after. The tribe that had called itself, with so little originality, The Originals, retreated into tunnels that had once carried water or borne express trains into the city. The tunnels grew into hives that were so tall, those who dwelt on the upper floors looked down on swirling cloudbanks drifting in from the advancing shorelines. The generation that had been despised by their own parents began to die, but each in their own special way. Some of the men expired while idling on their enormous motorcycles in the hallways. There seemed to be some children but they were never seen. Sometimes you could hear their voices echoing in the stairwells, Olly olly oxen free . . . come out . . . come out . . . wherever you are.

While You were Out

The last of the Neanderthals lay enthralled under the Constellation Virgo. It whispered in his ear, I told you so. A continent of melting ice dragged itself northward, leaving a mess of boulders, puddles and lakes on the plains. The White City allowed itself to be caressed by writhing, diaphanous cloud shadows, briers, brambles and poisonous vines. The clock struck twelve. While waiting for you I wrote a poem on a bar napkin. It went like this: The first time I saw you, it was The Library Fire. Everything I had ever known—everything anyone had ever known—up in flames.

Out

One potato two potato give me some skin Daddy-O.
A little dab'll do ya. My sister says, You make a better
door than a window. Delicious nutritious will make
you feel ambitious. How much is that doggy in the
window? We go in and out the window. I scramble
up the drainpipe to the rooftop. Catch me if you dare.
As we have done before. Where are you going? Out.
Where have you been? Out. Mom and Dad are the
see-through man and woman. We can take them apart
and put them back together again. When we take
Mom's heart out and open it, we find that it is lined
with satin that has been torn and shredded. Out went
the doctor. Out went the nurse. Out went the lady
with the alligator purse.

Tomorrow Days

Archie wants Veronica but dates Betty. Plastic Man's disguised as a lamppost. There's Mr. Dithers, all in a dither at Dagwood. He gives chase—Bumstead's toast. O Daisy Mae, please be mine. I love your ragged cut-offs. Bizarros in reverse time inhabit a square planet. These days of Dagwood and Blondie. Of Nancy and Sluggo lost in the forest. Grandma invites them to tea. These days when sandwiches are sandwiches. Old Mary Worth seems to live forever. Barehanded, Popeye pops open a can of spinach. The witch from the Chamber of Horrors beckons at the door to the crypt. The worms crawl in the worms crawl out. Her hook-hand, her basket of crumpets. Not today, Nancy says. Sluggo wants a crumpet. Maybe tomorrow.

To Market

Hickory, Dickory and Dock went to market. But the market was broken. It had a big fall. Or they had the wrong day. Hickory was wondering, What would all the king's horses know about putting anything back together again anyway? He was a natural leader and had planned the outing to the market. Dickory, who wore the red coxcomb and bells of the silly one, sat in the corner of an empty market stall. He said, If the market was not broken, we could buy blackbirds for a pie. Dock was the smart one. You could depend on Dock. He wore wire-rimmed glasses. He would know how to put something back together again. Dock said, We all have to go home now, all the way home.

Like a Crooked Man

Like a broken banister over a broken stairway. Like thistles blown across a parking lot. Like flakes of mother-of-pearl encased in mud. Like a glass door-knob. Like a shoe. Like an aluminum can wedged into the fork of a tree. Like a wet glove. Like a road sign in a ditch: Slow . . . Children . . . Playing. And here I am, not remembering the name of the wind that brought me here.

In the Door and Out the Window

One morning when he entered the tent he used as an office, he noticed an orange outdoor electric cord lying across the carpet. He knelt and took it in his hand. He stood holding it and realized it was not an outdoor electric cord but a thick vine. It ran in the entrance and out a hole in the rear of the tent. He gave it a gentle tug, then harder. Wherever it came from, wherever it was going, the attachment was strong. He almost expected it to tug back in response to his tug. What would it do if he pulled as hard as he could? He set it down. He thought of getting the garden clippers. But what if he cut the vine and it shrieked in pain?

The Promise

The bear did not return as he had promised and the tree refused to grow. The boy waited for the bear in the cottage. While he waited, he refused to grow older. Grandma decided to cut the tree down. She swung her axe into its bark and it bled. She decided to leave the tree alone. The boy dreamt that he was the only one who knew the answer to the riddle of the three: The bear, the cottage, the tree. Or was it the star, the crossroads, and the three words to say? Grandma died and the boy was alone. He set off to find where everyone had gone. When he looked back at the tree, it had grown much taller.

The Unmentionables

Lost at Bloomingdale's, the boy wanders. He finds himself in Lingerie among the unmentionables. The Unmentionables—that is what Grandma calls them. He imagines them as a band of heroes, dandyish crime fighters dressed in silk and taffeta. They go on unheralded missions and face unspeakable horrors with wit and casual aplomb. They have a way of walking through the credits of each episode, together, all five of them, a certain devil-may-care stroll—yet, they would go unnoticed in a crowd. Now he rides the Down escalator on his way to the first floor. He will find a security guard who will take him to the manager, and the manager will give him a lollipop. There will be an announcement on the public address system: If you have lost a boy, please come to the manager's office on the first floor. On his way down he looks up, and across from him there is another boy who looks exactly like him on another escalator. He shouts and points, Hey, you look just like me! The other boy does the same. He realizes the entire wall is a mirror and laughs. The other boy laughs too. They smile at each other as they descend on their separate journeys.

Room Seven

After months of little activity, the patient realized that the room was not solid, and that it was possible to fly. The successive walls of the cubicles seemed to slow him down, but he did penetrate the building without too much effort. Once outside, he skimmed somewhat awkwardly over the fence and rose into the sky. Canyons, cliffs, a castle and moat, towers, flags, and a standard sunset were provided. Also a forest with a winding path, appropriate obstacles, and a guardian disguised as a wretched old beggar.

Bring Back

Bring back the rolltop desk. Bring back inkwells. And ink, and fountain pens. Don't bring back Mrs. Tucker, my fourth grade teacher leaning over me as I practice my penmanship. Bring back the letter that comes in the mail. The one from a famous poet that says, Surely, you will be a famous poet. Bring back the dropped glove. Bring back slapping your rival's face with the glove that you slip off your hand with a certain panache. Bring back panache and the duel at dawn, and while we are at it, bring back minions to do my bidding and fainting on a couch and swooning and the swooning couch and falling in love with a stranger for all eternity. And eternity. Whatever happened to eternity? Bring back eternity.

The Aloha Shirt

If the light was divided from the darkness, why was it light and not lightness? That seems out of balance somehow. But it was good. Is that why you can't decide about the Aloha shirt? You slide them along the rack, parting the dark from the light. Separating a jungle under a full moon from dolphins leaping in the sunlight. Rather than quiet division, maybe it was more of an explosion, and God, who had been everything and everywhere, forever and never, was shattered into pieces. Like the pineapples falling through the red background on one of your Aloha shirts that have often been mistaken for hand grenades. You don't need the Aloha shirt with the ocean liners, and put it back on the rack. You don't need your books, not your fedora nor Greek fisherman's cap, not your bed, not the dust under your bed, nor the station wagon with flat tires on your front lawn. What if God was not God but a minor god or Satan, and the universe and all its creation was so much excrement? You don't want it, don't want to touch it, not with your skin or your body or even your thoughts. What if there are fragments of God scattered everywhere? Even the prisoners in the orange jumpsuits picking up garbage along the road, and the road and the empty bottles and garbage bags were all God? Like the way you fold your Aloha shirts when winter comes. Putting things back on the shelves, picking up, folding the Aloha shirts, the one with the martini glasses you like to wear to parties, the one with the bamboo grove, the one with Mustang convertibles, the hibiscus flowers, the one that is all black, the solid white one you wear to weddings. Putting them all back. Putting everything back where it belongs.

The Immortals

They do not know what time is. Birth is like saying goodbye. They are born old. There is a ringing in their memories. As if they are late or early for an appointment. They remember the future. They can only die in a dream. They never take naps on couches. They fear the roarie-bummlers, the fast-moving cloud shadows. Their eyelids are transparent. They suspect that they do not exist. They do not know what time is. There is a ringing in their memories. They can only die in a dream.

Before

Before the great continental rift and the sun collapsing
in regret before regret collapsed into blame before the
ice fields folded into themselves, this was all during
the disasters during the nocturnal slinging of the
machete in the era of the forced hinge and its rusty
creaking, when the snowdrifts refused to drift and the
glass question marks, well, the less said of them the
better. Suffice it to say that all musical instruments
had to be tuned to one prologue. Before the prologue,
the warm-up, before genuflections of never and
forever, before I knew there was no way to pronounce
your unpronounceable name.

Dark Matter Here

Nothing new to report except the rain. K's new 'do glows silver. Rush hour brush-passes. We were not burned switching umbrellas. Mynah Bird wants a new babysitter. She may need to be retired. Successful starburst maneuvers at church. Doom Bell has taken to sleeping in his coffin again. The dead drop is dead. Control not responding to my dispatches. Much misinformation concerning my whereabouts from K. When I walk down the street no one follows. Only the blank stares of manikins in store windows. Nobody knows what I am, evie, ivy, over—evie, ivy, over.

Diorama

Black in a black mirror—the glass panther. Even if you do not dream—the glass panther. On top of the Philco radio, in front of the rabbit ears—the glass panther. The credenza, the Barcalounger, the Formica table, the orange vinyl barstool, the chrome bar caddy, matching martini shaker, the Sputnik lamp—the glass panther. A puddle of India ink on a white patio floor. Rousseau moonlight, the bullet-shaped planter, plastic spear-shaped leaves, Sky King pedal plane, the ancient starlight, the rhinestone eyes of the glass panther.

The Show

The first act of the show was called The Old Crone. It featured an old crone sitting in a rocking chair smoking a corncob pipe. The men in the audience were not pleased. They wanted a young crone naked in a wine vat stomping on grapes. Some people were lost among the tents and the hullabaloo, not to mention the folderol. But guess what, it was all part of the show and the next act was called Some People Lost. The men, who had been expecting an explosion, were not pleased. But then—drum roll—there was an explosion. This part of the show was called The Arrival of Space, Time, and Matter. But it was so brief, just a puff really, and there was suddenly *there,* where there had been no *there.* Big deal, one of the men said as he rose from his chair and left the tent. The next part of the show was the big finale. It was called Spanish Dancer, or How Many Doctors Did it Take? It ended with the smoke from the explosion slinking off into the night. Too slow, too slow for an explosion. The men who remained in the tent demanded their money back.

One, Two, Three Alary

What is alary? Maybe it is a place. A place where you can dance if you are a boy and no one will say, Boys don't dance. Even the boulders in Alary can dance in a bouldery way. Four, five, six alary. It is where oxen go when they are set free. So free, they erase themselves from history, and that means the movies. You never see oxen pulling a wagon train. You never see cowboys riding oxen, or an oxen stampede. You never see an ox go crazy after eating locoweed. If you are a boy in Alary you can skip and no one will say, Boys don't skip. Even if you are a dancing skeleton, bones all akimbo, in Alary no one will say, Bones don't dance. That is why the boys in Alary are wearing caps on their heads, and suspenders hold up their pants that are a little too big for them. That is why there is a newsboy on the corner calling Extra, extra read all about it. Why the girls are playing hopscotch. And Jane writes in her journal, See Spot run. See how he runs. And when night comes you can hear a child's voice in the distance calling Olly olly oxen free . . . olly olly oxen free. And the oxen are wandering off toward the empty lots, toward the fields of tall grass.

Porridge

The boy wondered what porridge was. He imagined it like Jell-O, in a domed shape, green, and somehow hot and shimmering. Later, when he could read on his own, he was disappointed to see that Goldilocks had been charged with breaking and entering. But the case was thrown out of court. Really, what judge would convict Goldilocks—her golden locks, her smile, the blue sparkle in her eyes? The bears promised a civil suit. But nothing came of it. People forgot about the bears. And the bears, who had returned to the forest, may have liked it that way. They refused all interviews forever after. Speaking of after, when the boy saw the Emerald City of Oz for the first time, glowing in the distance, he remembered his concept of porridge . . . how silly it seemed. It was, after all, only oatmeal.

RICHARD GARCIA won the 2016 Press 53 Award for Poetry for *Porridge.* He is the author of seven books of poetry, recently *The Other Odyssey,* from Dream Horse Press, and *The Chair,* from BOA Editions, both published in 2014. His poems appear in many journals, including *The Georgia Review* and *Spillway,* and in anthologies such as *The Pushcart Prize* and *Best American Poetry.* He lives in Charleston, South Carolina with his wife Katherine Williams and their dog Max. He is on the faculty of the Antioch University Los Angeles MFA in Creative Writing program.

CPSIA information can be obtained at www.ICGtesting.com
Printed in the USA
BVOW08s2124250316

441437BV00013B/33/P

9 781941 209356